Gallery Books
Editor: Peter Fallon

MISERY HILL

David Wheatley

MISERY HILL

for Tony
with best wishes
David Wheatley

Gallery Books

Misery Hill
is first published
simultaneously in paperback
and in a clothbound edition
on 16 November 2000.

The Gallery Press
Loughcrew
Oldcastle
County Meath
Ireland

ISBN 1 85235 277 9 (*paperback*)
1 85235 278 7 (*clothbound*)

The Gallery Press acknowledges the financial assistance
of An Chomhairle Ealaíon / The Arts Council, Ireland,
and the Arts Council of Northern Ireland.

Contents

for Justin Quinn

Early Start

The grizzled one we meet in the hall,
the out of work painter, is pacing the floor
of the room overhead, up early or not gone to bed yet.
That was your bicycle he tripped over,
cursing noisily when he came in. Today
as usual he will knock during breakfast
in search of change for the phone and some milk.
The scratching under the sink
went quiet again around the same time:
your cupboards have nothing they want,
whatever they are. The stars shade back
to invisible and the fire in the grate has dispersed
to a smoke signal lost in the rain,
leaving the room in its wake like a lungful
of tired air we have breathed in all night.
The meter's a petulant mouth I grope in the darkness
to feed; we shower ourselves clean of each other,
emerge dripping on lino that curls at the edges.
I use your brush on my teeth, cover this morning's
scrubbed frame with yesterday's clothes;
the radio wakes itself to the headlines at six,
and this, I know, is the good life: the slow fade-up
of the heater's Cheshire cat grin, a free gift
in the cereal packet, daybreak still as sharp
a surprise as the scalding first taste of the coffee.

Misery Hill

Miserere, Domine . . .

Streetsign gone and most of the street,
high walls asterisked with wire,
impassable rubble victorious:
only the allure of a name
still on the map but nowhere else.

A name on a map but even at that
more solid than so many other ghosts
I have stalked in our snap-together capital
of forgetfulness — Blind Alley,
Smock Alley, Hangman's Lane,

Isolde's Tower. Names fade,
people forget. I pick through the débris:
a pram, a tyre, a handbag. The wind
rises, five o'clock comes: cars
drift down the quay past Misery Hill.

Grey of a low sky that is not
debauched white or compromised black,
but as if in essence one
with the rubble and the circling gulls,
an ideal colourlessness called grey.

Only the gods that are cranes can see
the wreckers' yard behind one wall,
the warehouse roofs, the funnels and steeples
holding the sky aloft beneath
the low banked clouds in which they dissolve.

The gulls' cry mixed with a churchbell,
the horn from a freighter moored on the quay,
fade; traffic fades. The river
nearby, ebbed to a trickle and stinking,
is soundless: cry out and no one will hear.

Here's a single high-heeled shoe
posed upright, still wearable,
and a poster for a concert last year.
Might its owner come back for the shoe?
Is there still time to buy tickets?

The wind lifts again, a post-office van
passes silently by with letters
for anywhere but this grim street
with its rubble and wire-topped walls,
featureless and empty besides.

Sonnets to James Clarence Mangan

1

Fishamble Street, the Civic Offices
turning the sky a bureaucratic grey
above a vacant lot's rent-free decay:
craters, glass, graffiti, vomit, faeces.
One last buttressed Georgian house holds out
precariously against the wreckers' ball
or simply lacks the energy to fall
and rise again as one more concrete blot.
Ghost harmonics of the first *Messiah*
echo round the Handel Hotel and mix
with bells long redeveloped out of use
at Saints Michael and John's, a ghostly choir
rising and falling until the daydream breaks . . .
Silence. Of you, Mangan, not a trace.

2

While Dublin's 'mass of animated filth'
was being urged by Shelley to revolt,
a childhood slum, its beetles, damp and mould,
was loosening your flimsy grip on health.
An older brother mysteriously dead,
parents that you couldn't blame enough:
what better way to cast your home life off
than changing into someone else instead?
Of all the masks you donned, which one was you:
'An Idler', 'Peter Puff Secundus', 'M.E.',
'Selber', Shakespeare's 'Clarence', all or none?
Your self dispersed more than it ever grew,
a dizzy paper trail, your fate to be
a nation's anonym, 'The Nameless One'.

3

Green spectacles, a wigwam of a cape,
a huge fedora with the brim pulled down
combined to set the proper *maudit* tone
of ostentatiously stillborn escape:
Akakii Akakievich had yet to lift
a quill when you began the zombie slog
of scrivening that paid for board and grog
but cost you any daytime on your craft.
Of all the ink you spilt in Kenrick's York
Street office, what survives? A tonweight of
old ledgers somewhere still for me to find,
dust off and publish as your masterwork
with running commentary by some Prof
on every memo, slip and bill you signed?

4

Saved, scavenged for your mocking art
a few young loves more myth than fact, none
returned, make up your sum performance on
that 'perforated pump', the human heart.
Human loves, I mean: there was one other
hiding in your landscape of the lost,
disembodied as a famine ghost
but clinging, clinging to her poet lover
for dear death — that vamp Dark Rosaleen.
Gone in the teeth, her breasts dried up, with no
place but some ragged ballads to call home,
what desperate last chance could she have seen
in you to make her think your lines would sow
redemption in her cobwebbed, empty womb?

5

No more than I can, James, could you refuse
demands for instant copy from the press.
Unlike mine though, your verse paid; alas,
the only work I'm paid for is . . . reviews.
The post this morning brings a dreary load
of books for journalistic vivisection.
My inertia jumpstarts into action:
what, X still alive — and still no good?
Perhaps one day he'll make it to my shelf;
on form like this he should be glad he's skimmed
and not thrown out *before* the carve-up starts.
Help me, James, to take upon myself
the sins of poets: help me to tell the damned
and saved apart, all in eight hundred words!

6

If poetry wells up from some true source
Pierian spring water's all we need,
Pope innocently thought — who never tried
The Phoenix, Mulligan's, The Bleeding Horse.
What welled up there, an evening's work done,
were beer and whiskey streams to ease your drought,
overflowing, when your purse allowed,
to raging floodtides of oblivion.
Which lasts longer, poetry or drink?
Posterity's a cheque no barman yet's
agreed to change, and fame a low-class brothel.
And yet what better place than down the sink
for words, like streams, to find the sea, and what's
a poem if not a message in a bottle?

7

A pain as vivid as it left you numb,
anaesthetised by drinking only to
awake again, called for a killer blow —
called for sixty drops of laudanum.
Which pain no sooner died than resurrected
and needed killing one more final time
(each time always the last), and you'd become
a vampire and its hunter, both addicted
to the same cheap thrills, the same cheap fix
that dealers on streetcorners still dispense
today like snow — a snow that turns to slush
in blackouts, bleeding gums and unsafe sex,
the search among the wreckage of your veins
for a spot to stick the needle in and push.

8

. . . *Deliver us from evil.* I almost join
the tiny congregation — headscarved women,
a dog, some winos — in its terse *Amen*,
half hopeless affirmation and half groan.
The notices inside the porch remind
me of the prayer group and jumble sale,
the pilgrimage to Knock, and who to tell
about that pregnancy you didn't want . . .
James, for all your sinner's *grand guignol*
and tearful one-night stands with penitence,
your faith remained the same — in heresy,
the earthly kingdom of a 'ruined soul'.
I grace an empty poorbox with a tuppence:
Remembered in our prayers . . . Lord have mercy!

9

The moon clouds over, the alley-cats start to fight.
Witching hour: wan, distorted outcasts
of the next world and of this, your ghosts
come swarming round your oil-lamp's garish light.
Rows of bloodless hands outstretched they plead,
asking only prayers for their repose,
but scheming coldly, if you dare refuse,
to drag you down with them among the dead.
My occult powers can't compare with yours,
but it does say in this morning's horoscope
that opportunity is on the way:
my fate is in the hands of Dial Your Stars,
off-peak rates, I'm pinning all my hope
on Tarot One-to-One and Live Feng Shui.

10

An east wind unleashed in Siberia,
your land where 'nothing blooms', whips in from
the sea and quickly makes itself at home
outside my window in suburbia.
Spain, Prague, Russia . . . Stuck here all your days,
you conjured dream and nightmare worlds in rhyme,
but never pictured anything as grim
as row on awful row of semi-d's.
If only you like me had known the leafy
suburbs pastured on our mortgages
you could have forgone all your Shangri-las
to pioneer Siberia-sur-Liffey
in a brave new world of double glazing, hedges,
hose pipes, patios and second cars!

11

A folio creaks open, coughs a decade
of stored-up dust into your prying face.
Wrinkled, foxed, strong evidence of fleas . . .
the book itself is scarcely less decayed.
The race is on. Your poems gather speed,
realising time is running out.
And not for you alone: leaking rot,
the barren harvests run to barren seed.
But at your College desk your books retain
their unavailing charm, a Provost's bust
still pledges learning's universal salve.
That can no more save the land from ruin
than spare you that incalculable waste.
That spectacle. Your country left to starve.

12

A burger box and a burger too, a chipbox
and a milkshake bobbing in the fountain:
sustenance for your undernourished phantom.
Soapsud refill cans of Harp and Beck's.
The Eason's clock and Pro-Cathedral bells
chime a sacred-secular *Te deum*
on the hour to break the tedium
(real bells this time!) in busy streets and malls.
Evening Herald! . . . Roaring every word
a harmless case informs me Who is master,
and Who died for my sins to save the dayglo
giant foetus on his sandwich board.
Three for a pound, the cigarette lighters! . . . The poster
for a clearance sale reads: ALL MUST GO.

13

The yawning earth absorbs another guest.
A knot of mourners plumed in heavy crêpe
thins to a single hooded, female shape.
Then no one. Corpse to bone to soil to dust,
dust to dust, then even that much gone.
I skulk among Glasnevin's plaster Christs,
the well-kept gravel paths and nettle wastes,
the rows of plots in search of . . . here's the one.
IHS: *In hoc signo*, 'I have
suffered'? They blend like the rain and sodden earth
as the sun drowns. A few late rays hang on
to probe the fading script. *In memory of* . . .
No farce of flesh and blood but, given birth
to into death, MANGAN graved in stone.

14

Let the city sleep on undisturbed,
new hotels and apartment blocks replace
the Dublin that we brick by brick erase;
let your city die without a word
of pity, indignation, grief or blame,
the vampire crime lords fatten on its flesh
and planners zone the corpse for laundered cash,
but let your heedless cry remain the same:
'The only city that I called my own
sank with me into everlasting shade.
I was born the year that Emmet swung
and died my fever death in '49:
my words are a matchstick falling through the void
and scorch the centuries to come with song.'

Umbrellas

Suddenly up wherever rain is,
brash as circumflex accents,

tablecloth-patterned, tartan or plain,
rigged like crinolines, cruelly tipped,

nudging and shoving over our heads
as helpless, borne aloft,

as caged canaries down mines;
bellying, caught in the wind,

and almost indecent turned inside out
(bins a carnage of nylon and spokes)

but staying behind on buses and trains
on urgent business of their own:

the transmigration of umbrellas
from owner to owner and shower to shower

in search of a Flood that will never again
dry up but drown in its mercy the city

and all it contains, upturned umbrellas
floating free like only survivors.

Jaywalking

A busker plays the guitar left-handed;
my hands, carrying
a plastic bag and a paper,

have been reversed in the glass façade
my double advances from
to greet me crossing the road.

However I follow it,
his clumsy rush
to the kerb leaves me scarcely

time to keep up or remember:
is it on the left
or the right that cars drive here?

If there was a clock, alive
to the danger, the second hand
would have gone into alarmed reverse.

Now I'm surrounded,
stuck on the white line
in what feels like the last scene from

Invasion of the Body Snatchers,
eye to eye
with my passing reflection.

I rewind to your terse goodbye
of the previous night
('Watch yourself out there') —

like mirror writing
read in a mirror,
travestied into meaning at last.

Traffic

Drawing up to the traffic lights,
the amber's blushes deepening to red,
I'm tempted with the open road in my sights

and while I've got the revs
to throttle on regardless
through the crossroads,

the traffic just let loose,
and, stepping on it, flounce
to safety — assuming those

pedestrians
don't mind. If they take
theirs, I'll take my chance . . .

❖

. . . take my chance the brakes
on this machine still work. They ease
me to a halt without a squeak.

❖

Let's linger a while then under the gaze
of election losers' posters, of bra-ad
nymphs exquisite in gauze

and nothing else, of Brad
Pitt and Demi Moore,
of the Dulux dog's shaggy braids.

Let's linger a while and try not to stare
at the man in the car beside us
picking his nose, smooth our hair,

look for something good (oh what's the use)
on the radio, bite a nail, or just
breathe in the diesel perfume of the 84 bus.

❖

Let's watch the people filing past
and guess where they might be going,
the quick, the slow, the blind, the lost,

the students, the shoppers, the gang
of office girls off to a sandwich and
coffee for lunch, their greying

bosses to something more grand.
Let's watch the woman who pushes a trolley
stocked with whatever she's found

by the side of the road, the folly
of jaywalkers trying to dodge
the facing traffic, the carefully

hoisted leg of a dog overcome by the urge
to take a leak as it crosses the road.
My foot on the pedal releases a surge

of impatience: 'At this rate . . . '
At this rate of chewing, by rights,
your fingernail should be down to the root.

❖

Rev all you like though or idle in quiet,
you're as stuck in a Merc
as you are in a Ford or a Fiat:

rage, fume, pull over and park,
but don't assume you're getting out of here
before dark.

Train yourself in how to stay put:
learn from the pedal-powered
lycra lout

briefly at ease, the horse and cart
with a fridge, a ladder,
some kids and a kitchen sink on board,

the Seat, the Saab and the Škoda
whose dodgy exhaust
makes you shudder,

the old Jag restored at great cost,
the Nissan
that's a bucket of rust,

the ice-cream van
and the empty hearse,
and somewhere in all these cars your own —

all standing their ground in one giant pause
before the handbrakes come off
and we disperse . . .

❖

to various urgent ports of
call: to Blackrock, Greygates and Whitehall,
Valley View and Meadow Grove,

Paradise Place, Misery Hill,
Rosary Terrace, Protestant Row,
Bray Head and Curly's Hole,

affordable suburbs (showhouses on view),
a comforting hearth,
an empty house or a bedsit for two

in the Dunes, the Elms, the Gallops, the Garth,
and other assorted
ends of the earth.

Let's serve our time and take the first shortcut
to any and every place
you want, let's leave it for dead, this sordid

paralysed town, let's cut loose
to wherever a car
can go on half a tank of unleaded gas.

❖

Red becomes green. Your trip starts here.

Final Call

In a place that is scarcely a place,
between two railway tracks,
down an underpass

or along the hard shoulder
on the airport road,
I'm making my way

in an all-weather mac
and laceless trainers. Don't
stop me or ask where I'm bound.

I'll know when I get there.
Until then I carry
a list of names and addresses,

all crossed out,
a blank passport,
an empty suitcase in both hands.

❖

When his briefcase spills open
the old woman sitting beside him
on the Heathrow shuttle

stoops to help the accountant
gather his papers, his calculator,
his pornographic magazine.

❖

You stumble on
a cleaning lady polishing
on all fours,

a sign on the door
behind her that reads
'Do Not Open This Door'.

❖

An old priest struck
by the ring of last, of terminal
things to it all

as he dawdles to pick up
a bottle of duty free
before the final call.

❖

I am the lost child whose name
you mishear on the PA,
whose parents are requested

to pick up the nearest
courtesy telephone
if they are still in the building,

still looking for me,
or if I am really lost
and not just another departure
misheard among all the rest.

❖

The girl beside you
at the sandwich bar

in a sleeveless top,
a tattooed heron
on her shoulder,

not suspecting
how it stretches its wings
in slow, methodical beats

as she lifts a hand
to smooth her hair
and put on a Walkman:

how any second now,
silently, slowly,
the bird will have flown.

An Apple Pip

I'm tricycling in circles round the old orchard
when my grandmother calls me in from the front door.
Her lined hands, when she waves, are covered in flour.
There will be salad for dinner, cake afterwards,

then time doled out by a ceremonial ancient
clock in the living room with the tea and talk,
the smell of antimacassars and cigarette smoke
and the glass of barley water I never want

but still am given. Windfalls lie thick on the ground.
The trees are stooped by the weight of their neglect,
apples that no one has bothered to collect
again this year and that crumble to mush in the hand.

My grandmother is icing the dessert
as I meet my grandfather lumbering from the shed
to a chair at the fading tablecloth inside
and a muttered grace before the meal can start.

The kettle's smoking gun as it pours out a refill:
Sunday after Sunday every week
the same performance played out, so alike
each Sunday, so unchanging it could still

be going on and I still five years old
but for the moment when a future counted
on to stay like this gets lost, upended
into pastness and the memory of a child;

the bicycle careering into a nettle-
patch in the orchard, the burning and the stink
of liniment rubbed on where I've been stung,
and after that no going back to the saddle

unless to cycle backwards from now on,
out of the tangled roots and the nettle-trap,
back to the original apple pip
into which I gather all that's grown

and gone and give it all a second chance;
my long-dead grandparents restored to life,
a beetroot salad I pretend to like,
the windfalls falling upward to the branch.

Moonshine

The ball dribbles off the green and into the drink.
My round at Druid's Glen isn't going too well.
A man in ridiculous trousers eyes up a putt.
Afterwards there will be G & Ts all round.

❖

My great-grandfather, the steward, is doing the rounds
on the Tottenham estate, the golf-course-to-be. Should he put
up a fence around it or brick up the old well
lest anyone fall down it into the drink?

❖

It's years now since the place was sold. They did well
out if it too, I was told once over a drink
by a Tottenham cousin of theirs (I get around)
who told me another story he had off pat:

❖

how an ancestor whose body was covered in weals,
poor man, lived on the same estate and used to put
wine in his bath, which his wily steward drained,
bottled, and sold for the unwitting locals to drink.

Chronicle

My grandfather is chugging along the back roads
between Kilcoole and Newtown in his van,
the first wood-panelled Morris Minor in Wicklow.
Evening is draped lazily over the mountains;
one hapless midnight, mistaking the garage door
for open, he drove right through it, waking my father.

The old man never did get to farm like his father,
preferring to trundle his taxi along the back roads.
Visiting, I stand in his workshop door
and try to engage him in small talk, always in vain,
then climb the uncarpeted stairs to look at the mountains
hulking over soggy, up-and-down Wicklow.

Cattle, accents and muck: I don't have a clue,
I need everything explained to me by my father.
Clannish great-uncles somewhere nearer the mountains
are vaguer still, farming their few poor roods,
encountered at Christmas with wives who serve me oven-
baked bread and come to wave us off at the door.

My grandfather pacing the garden, benignly dour,
a whiskey or a Woodbine stuck in his claw,
a compost of newsprint in the back of his van.
You're mad to go live in Bray, he told my father,
somewhere he'd visit on rare and timorous raids,
too close to 'town' to be properly *Cill Mhantáin*.

All this coming back to me in the mountains
early one morning, crossing the windy corridor
to the Glen of Imaal, where schoolchildren read
acrostics to me of 'wet and wonderful Wicklow',
and driving on down to Hacketstown with my father
we find grandfather's grandfather under an even

gravestone gone to his Church of Ireland heaven,
and his grandfather too, my father maintains,
all turned, long since turned to graveyard fodder
just over the county line from their own dear Wicklow,
the dirt tracks, twisting lanes and third-class roads
they would have hauled themselves round while they endured,

before my father and I ever followed the roads
or my mountainy cousins first picked up a loy
or my grandfather's van ever hit that garage door.

Writer in Residence

I arrive in the classroom during Geography lesson.
Thirty tongues equally slow to loosen,
till a boy asks to read. I sit on a table and listen

to how a beast in calf on a neighbour's farm
took three hours to deliver but came to no harm.
Now the hands soar up, each child's 'I am'

proved aloud from the looping, unjoined script
that fills the flimsy copy-books they grip
and come the end of the year will mostly scrap

with hardly a second thought as they move on.
Who'll read to me then? I sit with them while I can.
They read and read long after the bell has gone.

BSE

On all sides of the open field lies terror,
the self you meet no matter where you run,
the empty sky your gone mind's perfect mirror.
We watch the wellied vet prepare his gun

and slip up from behind on your shy bulk.
The frail cords of lucidity cannot hold,
your teats still bulging with their useless milk
as the addled brain absorbs the mercy bolt.

At Sam McAllister's Grave

It was here they brought him, under a thorn tree
up a mile of brambled avenue, when
they buried McAllister in '99,

who chose to walk into the yeomen's fire
the night of the ambush, that Michael Dwyer
and his fellow renegades might go free,

who slipped away across the fields
as the dying man's blood spilt and spilt.

❖

McAllister's statue in Baltinglass,
defiant as that other man
of '98 whose statue I passed

each day in Wicklow town,
Billy Byrne, that 'man of great renown',
his outstretched hand,

such was his valiance,
raised not in surrender but defiance.

❖

Catching my thumb on a briar it trickled blood,
and putting it to my mouth I drank the blood
only for my thumb to trickle more blood
and more again, a tiny stream of blood;

and that same day as news of the carnage, the blood
in the streets began to come through, I thought of the blood
I had tasted and the streets awash with blood
so that a burst water main seemed a river of blood.

❖

Not that I could know, waiting one day
in the square for the bus, that a few miles up the road
the IRA, the 'real' IRA,
had jumped a Securicor van outside Ashford

before being jumped themselves on either side;
that just as an IRA man was pointing a gun
at a passerby's head
shooting began

and the Guards left him riddled, left him for dead
on the tarmac as his companions fled
through the fields, returning the Guards' fire as they went

and startling the cows in the long grass;
while I, a few miles down the road, impatient
for dinner, riddled what had become of the bus.

❖

But that day in Baltinglass, though I tasted my blood,
the only riddle was the riddle of blood
in the streets, somewhere a world away from the blood-
red wreath commemorating your spilt blood,

McAllister, in Baltinglass, where no blood
ran from murdered shoppers, and no more blood
flowed than from my thumb's pinprick of blood
that left on my tongue an innocent smudge of blood.

❖

And as for the man whose car was stopped,
an electrician on his way home,
once they'd decided not to take him
hostage, there being no reason to keep him trapped,

the raiders turned him free to blunder
down the road straight at the marksmen
leaving them to decide what his raised hands meant,
a gesture of defiance or surrender.

❖

And I thought, McAllister, not of your
heroic run or of your sacrifice
but of shoppers guided up the street

after the warning, to safety, they thought,
and what was waiting for them there,
and raising my hands against the sun

they burned blood-red before my eyes,
in Wicklow that August afternoon.

after Omagh, 16 August 1998

Poem

The roof has fallen but the house still stands.
Birds drop to our table from the open sky.
I cup and drink the rain from shivering hands.

Nothing could be simpler than my wants:
to go on living here not bothered why
the roof has fallen though the house still stands.

Some would assail the builders with complaints
(our bed was waterlogged last night). Not I,
cupping and drinking the rain from shivering hands.

You call it folly, I call it romance,
to weather each new test and still get by.
So what if the roof has fallen? The house still stands

and we still thrive in the muck and damp like plants,
nourished by the forces we defy.
I cup and drink the rain from shivering hands

and lie in the dark. The sea breeze roars and rants.
Drive us out? I'd like to see it try.
The roof has fallen but the house still stands.
I cup and drink the rain from shivering hands.

Table Manners

The arguments starting earlier each time,
over coffee, dessert, the meal, the wine,

their evenings drifted into slow reverse:
trysts became appointments, chores and worse,

the nothing that they had to lose they lost
in selfish mental tots of what it cost

calling for the bill and tipping too much
rather than wait a moment more to catch

not even the last or second last bus home,
or rather, the separate homes they started from

and that had failed to lead to somewhere else;
the dinners abruptly stopping and the calls —

as simple, the realisation it couldn't work,
as crossing and uncrossing a knife and fork.

The Door

after Simone Weil

Open the door to us and we'll see the orchards,
we'll drink their cold water printed with the moon.
Strangers' feet burn as the road leads onwards.
Ignorant, we seek a place and find none.

We want to see flowers? The drought here never ends.
Here we are, sick with waiting in front of the door.
We'll break it down, if needs be, with our hands.
We rush, we storm it: it's we who fall on the floor.

We have to draw breath, wait and look on helpless.
We look at the door intransitively sealed,
all eyes on it, weeping for our loss.
Still we look and the hours slip by; we've failed.

We face the door. Remind me, what do we want?
Nothing we won't be better off without.
We'll never get in. The door stands firm, an affront.
. . . The door opened, letting such silence out

that neither orchards nor one flower appeared,
only a space of light and empty waste
was suddenly everywhere, filling the heart
and washing our almost-blind eyes with its dust.

Goldfish

They've awful memories, she told me once:
each tour of their bubbling tank erases the last,
the excitement of five seconds ago dissolved
into the irretrievable goldfish past —

how many memory spans ago was it,
I wonder, watching her watch goldfish now,
old woman who sees a stranger's face in the glass
mouthing with twitching lips a silent *Who?*

Fireworks

Teenagers spilt from the pubs, all over each other,
men in football jerseys tight over paunches,
families out late, gorging on burgers and chips,
all make their way past the amusement arcades,
the buntinged kiosks, the bandstand and the aquarium
to mill on the promenade, and watch while the boat
moored fifty yards offshore kills its engine
and lights, and we know this is it, and at last it comes:
the countdown over a rackety PA
we all join in with and the splitsecond fear
that nothing is going to happen before the first
triumphant millefiori of gunpowder
explodes against the cool night sky to the tune of
The Ride of the Valkyries and the child beside you
bursts into tears and asks to be taken home.

Two Posthumous Sonnets

1 THE SANCTUARY LAMP

after Corbière

Sleep, it's all yours, your coffin bed. Don't bother
about the early worm. There's no new day
for you to greet: you're not you, but another.
Dream: true loves are always the furthest away . . .

Sleep, straddle the rays of the stars you unhook.
In the darkness of twilight your guardian angel
on the ceiling — a spider — will drop from his nook
and tie you up from every conceivable angle:

a morbid veil but one they'll lift tomorrow
as you lie in state, for a goodbye kiss.
So close your eyes, get ready for — what's this —

a thurible across your nose goes *Thump*!
You swell up like a sexton, full of marrow,
and glow all night like a sanctuary lamp.

2 A RUBIK'S CUBE

after Nemo Loris

I lost a lot more than my life, the afternoon
I died in Budapest, but what I miss most
are the colours: that shade
of Tokay we drank one day on the river,

your underwear showing when you walked over
a laundry vent in Oktogon,
the melt of your breakfast cheese on my toast
in mine or your flat (remind me again who paid

the rent), the fourteen Heroes' coppery smiles,
the Lukács hot-tub disturbed by my carefree plunge
and the sun through a skylight on the tiles . . .

piecing them all together now that I'm dead
like some sort of puzzle, or Rubik's cube: the orange,
the blue, the green, the yellow, the white and the red.

The Tone

drifting to sleep and reaching for her hand with his
he wades out into the glassy lake and wading in
over their heads together they sink and sinking
together tangled in weed think nothing of drowning
but still in the background faintly from somewhere comes
the sound of a telephone ringing or rather

restless in sleep and clutching her hand in his
they jump from the window-ledge on which they are sitting
and tug and tear at the wings of numberless birds
as they fall and keep falling and never arrive
at the ground so far below and still in the background
comes the sound of a telephone ringing or rather

deep in sleep her hand fallen open in his
they are carried along the empty streets of a city
that might be unpopulated they are carried in sleep
to an empty room in which a telephone rings
unanswered and says to no one in particular
sorry there's no one here at the moment speak after the tone

Recklessness

Join me again, love, in the old mistake,
that two share more than spittle in a kiss.
Don't think skin on skin will cure the ache,

the thirst you burn with and no kiss can slake.
But don't draw back. Lean close and whisper this:
join me again, love, in the old mistake,

you by whose warm side I choose to wake —
you too for all our insulating bliss
don't think skin on skin will cure the ache.

But *ache*? Why all the fuss? Why not just fake
the permanence we aim at and we miss?
Join me again, love, in the old mistake

that time will keep on giving and not take,
the more we love not leave us less and less.
Don't think skin on skin will cure the ache,

since ache it is, the compromise we make
each time we say — again now, say it, please —
'Join me again, love, in the old mistake.
Don't think. Skin on skin will cure the ache.'

B & B

It takes two or three flushes
to make them vanish,
our latex jellyfish,
discarded after the act

on the pile of *Hello* magazines
by the bed, spoiling the musk
of the pot-pourri and, already,
the artery-thickening smell

of the fry from down the corridor:
like the sign says, BREAKFAST
WILL NOT BE SERVED AFTER LUNCH.
And the peremptory guidebook:

'Nothing to detain you
in this anonymous town.'
We phone ahead, cancel all plans,
stay for the rest of the week.

Miranda

Who is hiding from whom, you or the world
beyond your seacoast issueless as Bohemia's?
Not that the spell has failed, but has worked too well:
discarded chesspieces knee-deep in sand
along a beach lacking only the flagpoles and pier
to pass for an out-of-season Courtown or Bray,
your tights and blouses hung out to dry between
two trees while gibbering Caliban scowls at his pool,
the magical commonplace long since become
commonplace magic. Miranda, I've had enough too:
let me surprise you by failing the next time I try
to conjure a playing card from behind your ear
or an egg from your palm. Behind a shifting sand dune
that you pass every day and have never explored
my life-boat is waiting patiently for you,
and waiting in the long grass a suitcase packed
for your departure to somewhere disenchantingly
new in ways you could only marvel at now.

The Meaning of Summer

so it stinks, so the black plastic bags behind
the takeaway have been rifled by dogs again

that's my idea of summer
if it weren't for the cars we wouldn't
know what to do with the acres of tarmac

the helicopter's noise overhead
only makes straining to hear you across our table
out on the terrace all the sweeter

that's my idea of summer
not being able to walk down
the street for the crowds

but you can't have a drink, not until
you've jostled a few more shoppers
or spent the afternoon sweating at work
re-inking the photocopier

that's my idea of summer, what's yours?
here you are at last in O'Neill's

trying to get the barman's attention
here you are ordering overpriced food
in a restaurant that was a shoeshop last week

and next week will be a boutique
writing a fictional name and telephone number
on a matchbox for a stranger
at the next table and taking

a late bus home through street
after street of immaculate houses
where life has never been better

the moon in the clear sky inspiring
neither acknowledgement nor

despair merely the thought of how —
your shirt wringing wet by now —
you will sleep in your smell

without washing and be grateful
that's my idea of summer
how it gets almost unbearable
here but still worth it

Charm

I snap shut the notebook and put the pen aside.
The lines will never come, the garden needs work.
Suffice for me, morning coffee,
morning paper, now in this moment of doubt:
confirm, resume whatever it is
that starts again when words run out.

Misery Hill

for Caitríona

1

Fresh water lapping between my fingers again,
the city lights like the sky turned upside down:
the underworld behind us, gone now, gone!

We drifted past the Kish still waiting for dawn,
helpless before the unfamiliar stars.
Was this really the town I'd called my own?

Nemo didn't know. We traded stares.
I'd nothing to declare and nothing to lose.
Crag-like on the quay, a bearded tar

hailed us as we bumped into the shallows:
'That hulk of yours is only good for scrap.
Passports please.' Before I could cut loose,

'Is that a shadow I see?' the old tar snapped.
'Sorry, dead souls only on Misery Hill.'

2

He looked like he was serious too. I slipped

him a tenner. 'Happy holiday from hell,'
he waved us on. We queued in the café for breakfast.
The place was, in Nemo's words, 'a bit of a hole'.

My appetite for this tour was fading fast,
not to mention for the soggy chips.
A freighter inched laboriously past

the window into dock. Someone let slip
it was carrying a haul of contraband.
I watched the teeming crew secure the grips

and the first containers touch down on dry land.
The old tar knocked on one and yelled a testy
'Port of origin?' at the nearest deck-hand.

From somewhere inside the box came: '*Bucureşti*'.

3

I looked round for Nemo, but the café was awash
with what I took for a troupe of New Age crusties

all looking (and smelling) like they could do with a wash.
I could have done with one too: we stank to high heaven.
Nemo reappeared, bearing a toothbrush

and soap. 'How could you,' he began, 'even
imagine I'd leave you?' One of the new arrivals
yanked his jacket and asked, was this a safe haven

or what, and why did all the deck-hands have rifles?
It turned out my crusty friend was a Kosovar.
The week he'd spent as a stowaway sounded awful:

'It was as much as I could do to cross over.
The sailors spat at me, called me a dirty Arab.
Remember me, if you find her, to my daughter.'

4

Nemo passed me the streetmap, looking perturbed.
'I thought you knew where it was.' 'I thought *you* did.'
We walked a mile up the street and sat on the kerb

like a couple of bums, to be strictly avoided
or given the brush off: 'Never heard of the place . . . '
As we stood there looking for someone who had,

I heard the drone of an all-too-familiar voice:
'Sloth is of all passions the most powerful
passion . . . ' I interrupted: 'Don't you mean vice?

Get up and make yourself useful, Flemm, you old fool.'
Lying back in the gutter, he lowered his jaw
like a drawbridge, it took him so long: 'You never fail

to fail to amaze me. Useful? You're joking, I'm sure.
Now kindly stand out of the light while I scratch my arse.'

5

'How much more are you going to take of his craw-

thump?' Nemo asked. 'This clown is the least of our cares.'
But Flemm was as nothing to the sound and the fury
ahead, so deafening I stopped my ears

to the constant howls and shrieks of '*Miserere!*'
Pity, pity, I thought, they all want pity,
as if only they had ever suffered. I'm sorry,

but dead folk are ten a penny in this city,
or hadn't they noticed? One dead soul lumbered
forward, a wreck of what had once been a body.

'Every year you tourists get dumber and dumber,'
she groaned. 'We died by the bullet, the knife and the noose.
A helmeted man with a gun is all I remember

before I was shot, that day at Newlands Cross.'

6

The way they kept on coming it might have been
a lifetime's worth of cleaned-up TV news

spelt out for us in flesh, blood, gut and bone:
the HIV-positive addict kicked to death,
the contract hit, the body in the bin,

half eaten by dogs, the dealer robbed of breath
by block after concrete block dropped on his chest,
a screaming tabloid headline his only wreath.

'Not one screaming headline goes to waste,'
said Zozimus stepping up, Zozimus
we couldn't believe we were seeing, 'that saves the least

of these from being forgotten.' He presented us
with an ancient *Evening Herald*, more mould than paper.
'Make memory,' he added, 'your truest muse.'

7

I forget the rest. I wasn't prepared
for how fast daylight was ebbing away, and flicked
through the entertainment listings for something paupers

and deadbeats like us could afford. We were in luck:
there was a comedy night at a club on the quays.
Nemo paid in, and standing there on the look-

out for seats near the bar I found myself up close
with the star turn himself. 'I'm a great admirer
of yours,' I began, 'but why play a ghost-town like this?'

It was what he'd been waiting for: 'Maaara!
Not many people know this, but I have family
in these parts going back to Brian Boru,'

he growled, 'not to mention the O'Rahilly,
Cromwell, Saint Patrick, Strongbow and Molly Malone.'

8

While I stood there enjoying his homily

the noise of a helicopter coming down
got closer and closer until I lost the plot.
'Traffic has been reduced to a single lane

on the Naas dual carriageway,' said the shaken pilot.
'The city is fogbound.' It was AA Roadwatch.
'We're lucky,' his co-pilot said, 'we didn't go splat.'

'Plot?' asked Minos. 'Another plot being hatched
to haul your man in front of a tribunal?
Count me in: about time that snake was scotched.'

'All your dirt on him is so much balls,'
said Rashers. 'I'll see to it, if you're picking a fight,
that you and your honourable friend are blackballed:

I'll see to it you leave town on the next flight.'

9

He had to shout over the bar-talk and karaoke.
When the woman at the next table asked for a light

I thought: escape route. It was time to get plucky.
I gave her fifteen minutes of charm before
I asked could I sleep on her couch. She said OK.

I was out of there and slamming the door
almost but not quite fast enough to lose Nemo.
In the end *I* was the one who slept on the floor.

They woke me at dawn, cold as an Eskimo.
Hang on, this wasn't the room from after the pub!
Where was this place? Then, to my mounting trauma,

a key turned in the door. I felt someone grab,
bundle me out and punch me seven times.

10

‘Are we . . . are we there yet?’ I asked with a sob.

The warden was disgusted. ‘In your dreams,’
said Nemo. We followed the warden out to the stairs.
‘We could take the lift,’ he said, ‘but for your crimes

we walk.’ Crimes? We walked and walked for hours,
but only I got tired; when we got to the top
my feet had broken out in running sores —

or crawling sores more like. Rising up
in front of me was a wall of marble white.
‘If you were as pure as that, you scurvy pup,

as spotless clean, you wouldn’t have to wait,
you’d go straight up. But all you do is loaf.
It’s like you’re carrying some hidden weight:

the sin of pride, not “Pride (In the Name of Love)”.’

11

'The Lord upholdeth all that fall,' he went on,
'and raiseth up' — pause for thundering laugh

(what was so funny?) — 'all those that be bowed down.'
A photographer stepped forward to get me on film —
the first illumination, I thought, to dawn

on me so far. 'I don't get much work in this slum,'
he said. 'You're the first new story in years.
I trust you're familiar with *The Daily Flam*,

that knocking shop for toothless old media whores?'
'We were photographed leaving Le Coq Hardi,'
one interrupted. 'I felt for his wife, of course.'

'I was seen,' another said, 'at a party
with a former Miss Ireland. I never threw
that punch though. At most a glass of Bacardi . . . '

12

'Is there much more of this left to wade through?'
I asked Nemo. I didn't just mean the harangues:
I was ankle-deep in their mugshots too,

faded clippings of all their former swank,
magazine pages . . . the swill of long-dead glamour
overflowing like a septic tank.

How the mouthy were fallen! So much for *amour*
propre I thought, until I saw an entry
from my diary. It hit me like a hammer.

'Constant quarrels. Feel like leaving the country.
Christ, what a nuisance.' When I looked up, 'Confess,'
said Nemo. 'Or maybe that passes for gallantry

by your standards.' I confessed to his face.
Nemo smiled an imperceptible smile.

13

Looking back, I allowed my eyes to feast

on how far up we'd come from the foot of the hill.
'What a view,' said a voice in the breeze. I looked round:
no one. 'You have a good time. I'll pick up the bill.'

'What bill?' I'd just begun when, 'Rant rant rant!'
said Hera, 'that I could have dealt with, insults,
taunts, but it's the kindness I can't stand —

round here, the drippy philanthropy assaults
and lifelines reeling in the deserving stray.
I was envy incarnate and felt no guilt.

I wanted her dead. Given,' I heard her say,
'a wish, but on condition that she got twice
what I did, I'd ask . . . I'd ask to go blind in one eye.

And now I'm meant to forgive her like a big wuss?'

14

The wind
blew 'Yessssss!'

but I felt cut up. I felt drained.
'Get this man a cappuccino,' said Butthead
butting in, 'or should that be a "point

of Hoineken?" Huh huh.' I told him to beat it.
'He said "Beat it",' said Beavis. 'Who's a wuss now?
He wants a jerk-off.' I refused to be baited

but he went on: 'Aren't you going to show
us round town, "DORT" boy? It's one big wussorama
round here from Dalkey Island to the Red Cow.'

'And beyond,' said Butthead. 'They have, like, farmers,
grass, slurry and stuff, and I'm, like, "Duh",
like, "Where's my cappuccino?" Total bummer.

It sucks. They have, like, sheep, huh huh.' 'Huh huh.'
'Beavis, you're sitting on the remote again.'

15

Barring the way (I could have laughed) was a ha-ha.

The hook of a crane dropped from the sky: 'Going
up?' a voice invited. We both grabbed hold.
'Nemo,' I said, 'I've been thinking . . . ' 'Go on.'

'Tell me this search of ours hasn't ground to a halt.
Where's it leading? What's Flemm waiting for?
Who shot that woman? I demand to be told — '

'Hello, hello, caller on line four?'
the radio hissed. 'Hello? I've never heard
such whining. No wonder he hasn't got anywhere.

Perhaps he'd like me to hold his hand? The coward.
I demand he be told that he makes me sick.'
'Calm down,' said the DJ. 'Let me read your cards.'

Then the lights went off. But no one was hitting the sack.

16

I entered . . . *a waking trance . . . I saw the Hanged Man . . .*
all foreknown . . . foresuffered . . . for Christ's sake. . .

our affair . . . all rigged . . . each kiss, curse and moan! . . .
The comedy of it . . . love is of all passions
the most powerful . . . human love, do I mean? . . .

most powerful passion . . . but lost . . . I lost it . . . my patience
with her . . . jealousy . . . my feelings for her . . .
the other, I mean . . . not her . . . not Pia . . . all ancient

history . . . the nets of Calypso's hair . . .
unravelled years ago . . . and yet she'd ask
was she my substitute, my stand-in, my whore . . .

'Your willpower,' said Geulincx, 'has been reduced to a husk.
You want to drag her down to your shitty level.
Take off your hypocrite face and show us your mask.'

17

The trance . . . coming out of the trance . . . I felt awful.
Nemo handed me an unsigned letter.
'You have been warned,' it read, 'don't make us get lethal.

Watch yourself, scumbag.' We noticed an escalator
with 'Stairway to Heaven', the boyband version, playing
upstairs. I'd deal with the warning business later.

Or maybe I wouldn't. Why not, I wondered, just plonk
ourselves down up there, open some cans and smoke
some weed? I felt my mind go deliciously blank

and flopped to the ground. Nemo planted a smack
on my face. 'Stimuli, you want stimuli?
What's it to be: grass, coke, acid, smack?

I know what you want. You just want — ' 'That's a lie.'
I wasn't going to let him say it. Not yet.

18

What made me think that this way Pia lay?

'My Aim is True,' I whistled. But couldn't she wait?
Sloth is not sloth that alters when it finds
some piffling reason to give up my seat.

'Then let me not to the marriage of true buffoons,'
said Nemo, 'admit impediment. That tart
from the bar perhaps: she'd suit you down to the ground.

But Pia?' (He said it.) 'Why bother? Perhaps you're too tired?'
'First one step, then another, then millions more,'
said Zeno, 'all leading where? Will the end never start?

Or has it happened already?' 'We've been here before,'
Eubulides said. 'Why *should* there be a scheme
to all this?' As I got to my feet I swear

I heard myself whistle Coltrane's 'A Love Supreme' . . .

19

Those unfamiliar stars had scratched into view
overhead again. Time not for a trance but a dream.

And there she stood. Hair: Tawny. Eyes: Off-blue.
Features: Mobile. Instep: Available on
request. Moustache: *Moustache*? 'The fishnets suit you,

Nemo. Are those breasts plastic or your own?'
He ripped them off. 'So, the obscure object
of your libido lets you down again?

Is the Pope a — ' 'Yes,' said the Pope, 'he is, in fact.'
'Point proved,' said Nemo. 'You don't know what you want.
You don't want Pia, you just want in the abstract.'

'I had that problem once,' said the Pope. 'I went
through that whole "Young People of Misery Hill
I luff you" phase. Get real, son: drop the cant.'

20

I cant, I cant, I can't . . . I rallied the will-
power to get to my feet. We accepted a CD
('in Latin!') from the Pope and bade him farewell.

Slumped at a PASS machine we found a seedy
type who claimed to be Brian Boru. 'They've stopped
my pension,' he said. 'Offshore accounts, shady

deals, brown envelopes: I take the rap
while all my bastard tiger cubs get rich.
You couldn't spare any change? I'm royally strapped . . . '

I flung him a copper but before he could catch
it the ground beneath our feet took a violent heave,
flinging us well beyond the scrounger's reach.

'What was *that*?' I asked my guide. 'Believe
it or not,' he said, 'there's been a seismic shift.'

21

The crowd on the hillside gave a Mexican wave

and traders started selling earthquake T-shirts.
The atmosphere was like a carnival.
A passerby told us: ‘It’s not the close shave

we’re celebrating; we don’t mind the upheaval.
Round here we consider earthquakes good luck.
“Tiger burps”, we call them. They shorten travel

time too: there’s nothing like one when you’re stuck
on a rock-face or some other tricky corner.’
‘Mangan, is that you?’ I was taken aback.

‘I prefer to go under the persona
of The Nameless One,’ he said, ‘in homage
to my great hero, the shadowy loner . . .

Nemo! I’ll be damned if you’re not his image.’

22

‘No, I’ll be damned,’ said Nemo. ‘Let’s go have lunch.’
We found a cybercafé that seemed all the rage

with the raging palates within and Mangan launched
into a mountainous smoked ham and pesto panini,
then badly overtipped the buxom wench

of a waitress. ‘Outside the body of this skinny
wreck,’ he said, ‘is a glutton trying to get in.
The coffee here’s almost as good as in Nini’s.’

He e-mailed the counter for another one
while I picked an apple up from a bowl of fruit
for dessert, only for my teeth to close on

a mouthful of circuit boards. Not my kind of byte.
Perhaps it was an art exhibit or something.
We left in a hurry when I’d spat the thing out.

23

When all the beggars saw Nemo still chomping
his sandwich they crowded round in search of some crumbs.
If I was that wasted, I'd have done the same thing.

I'd never seen such a pack of underfed tramps.
'It's a disgrace,' said Yerk, 'an utter disgrace.'
I was about to agree when, 'Tits and bums,'

he said, 'wherever you look they're in your face
(as it were), tits and bums. I blame the media.
No decency left. I ask you! Women these days.'

A woman walked by. 'There, you get the idea?'
he asked, admiring her rump. 'Nudge nudge, wink wink,
say no more.' Could this place get any seedier?

We left him muttering to himself as we slunk
away: 'Condoms . . . divorce . . . abortion . . . Late Late Show'.

24

He followed us though (I must be a soft touch for cranks):

'You wouldn't say an auld prayer before you go?'
he asked, crossing himself. 'For whose intentions?'
I asked. 'For the souls in bliss.' 'Why not?' said Nemo.

'A prayer that short could hold even my attention.'
We looked round for Yerk to start but he'd disappeared.
'My sandwich has too,' said Nemo. A beggar sat munching

it in a doorway, wiping his mouth on his shirt.
Another apple fell on my head from a tree.
'I think this calls for a poem,' said Dingdong the bard,

clearing his throat: 'O sandwich, o apple . . . ' The three
of us legged it towards an orange glow up ahead.
Our tormentors had finally stooped to poetry.

The glow was coming from some sort of big black shed.

25

Behind the door we found a cackling floozie
who ushered us into the rave going on inside.

We couldn't see each other, the air was so hazy,
but all round us I could feel teeming flesh.
'They're not — ?' I asked Mangan. 'What's that you say?'

he shouted. Then it came to me in the flash
of a strobe light: everyone was having sex.
So Yerk was right about the local trash.

Somebody's hands were creeping up my legs,
male or female I couldn't see. A slime
of jism oozed underfoot. This wasn't the climax

I'd hoped for. Then I saw the bright orange gleam.
It was a fire blocking the way to the roof.
But we had to get through. We had to get through the flames.

26

We inched upstairs, fighting the gropers off.
'Sodomites! Zoophiles!! Procreators!!!'
Nemo screamed. But waiting up above

was Dingdong's *capo*. He too broke into verse:
'Squared off and seeable down through into,'
Omnibard said, as though pronouncing a curse.

'With a plinkety plonk of my hey nonny no
Elizabeth Bishop met Pele on the North Wall.
Snow-covered, Homeric poppies in Mayo,

Nerval in a Dutch interior in Kinsale.
The map of the hill is the map of a map of a map.
I was. A woman. In the suburbs. At nightfall.'

Mangan threw himself forward to shut him up.
Omnibard fell over and into the fire.

27

Not even furnace conditions could make him stop.

I could still hear his voice over the whir
of the helicopter blades from the roof outside.
A woman was gesturing to us from the far

side of the flames: it seemed we had a flight
to catch. 'After you,' said Nemo. I stepped
into the scorching, unbearable heart of light.

I couldn't even feel the tears I wept.
'I see her,' said Nemo. The fire was blocking my view
(who? who was it?). Then all of a sudden it stopped.

My rubber soles had melted — but we'd come through.
The check-in girl gave us an overnight bag
and told us to make a run for the chopper. Nemo

refused. 'I can't,' he said. 'I'm going back.'

28

I thought of chasing him but it was too late.
'Welcome on board,' said the pilot. 'Now please disembark.'

I must have crossed a time zone or slept through the flight.
'Welcome to the Paradise Place Experience,'
a soundtrack began in sync with the ambient light

slowly revealing 'City living at rents
you can afford' (the soundtrack again): mile
after mile of new apartment blocks where once —

the last time I checked — a muckheap covered all.
'"Rent" was to spare your sensitivities,'
an estate agent began through a cheesy smile.

'Unless you'd rather bid for a timeshare lease?'
I dipped my toe in a rock garden stream. The spray
from a fountain quivered exquisitely in the breeze.

29

My guide was keen I didn't get away
without the hard sell. 'Charming new period
residence,' she simpered, leading the way.

The wonders she promised left me starry-eyed:
'Needs total refurbishment but in pristine condition . . .
secluded city-centre location.' A riot

of bunting and streamers hung from the pebble-dashing
to greet me; loudspeakers blared out a welcome.
Teenagers helped old people hang out the washing,

offered to push their shopping trolleys home.
No litter or dog dirt anywhere to be seen,
playgrounds, parks . . . I couldn't but succumb.

This was the place for Pia and me. Then
I noticed a car coming. A stretch limo.

30

The ambient light dazzled from the windscreen.

The car drew up. A door opened: out came a
stream of minders with ear-pieces and shades.
I looked round — but this time there was no Nemo.

A leg swung out. Before she reached the heights
of a firm-set thigh, a second thigh and a pair
of lazy hips, this woman had gone to my head.

For it was she, torso and all: Pia.
'You've some nerve,' she said. 'Thought I'd give
you a second chance if you came crawling here?

I'll give you a second chance all right: to leave.
Sod off.' There must have been some grit in my eye:
I noticed it watering as I muttered, 'Forgive'.

The garden stream flowed decorously by.

31

Something more was called for I felt, so 'Cretin,'
I started, 'numbskull, gobshite, idiot boy . . . '

thumping my tub. I knew when I was beaten.
'Sorry, what's that?' asked Pia. 'Louder, please.'
The muscles in my throat began to tighten.

I just about managed some inarticulate pleas,
then as I made to step forward tripped in the stream.
'Now!' hissed my guide, 'tell her you're buying a place

here and she's yours.' Had these people no shame?
Her agency cohorts were handing Pia brochures
and raving about the crèche and the car-pooling scheme.

By now my sentence was clear: twenty years'
repayments. So I told her straight to her face.
'Allow me, Pia. If you want it, it's yours.'

32

The thought of how much she was going to fleece
me for sent my guide into raptures. Mangan
and Pia hopped for joy like a couple of fleas.

The children put up a maypole and danced round it singing.
Then she did it: 'And what do you intend
to use as collateral?' asked my guide. 'Hang on!'

I parried. Too late: I knew what was on her mind.
'I mean, you *can* pay for this?' Everyone stopped
dancing to look. 'Yes,' I said. 'Up to a point.'

Wrong answer. I stood there feeling pretty inept,
let me tell you. Then I heard something rumble.
The ground shook. There was nowhere to run; I was trapped.

It was the Tiger himself. I watched him trample
the maypole into the ground and assumed I was next.

33

His mistress Filthy Lucre surveyed the shambles

he'd made of the place and whooped. I was fixed
to the spot but as the monster moved in for the kill
it started to crackle and blur, like special effects

gone haywire, and not just the tiger: I watched the whole
thing fade, the apartment, the stream, the fountain, my guide,
and felt myself fall headlong through a black hole,

fall screaming all the way down the hillside
past Mangan, Nemo, Omnibard, Yerk and the rest,
to a bed in a Dublin bedsit, landing beside,

yes, Pia, lying stretched across my chest,
then waking and asking, 'You wouldn't have a coin
for the meter? I'll have a shower while you cook breakfast,'

and outside a few last stars and what looked like rain.

on Misery Hill brand-new carnation

Acknowledgements

Acknowledgement is due to the editors of the following publications, in which some of these poems have appeared: *Areté, Brangle, College Green, The Irish Times, New Hibernia Review, Nua, Papertiger, Poetry Ireland Review, The Recorder, ROPES, Southern Review, Stand, Thumbscrew, The Shop* and *Verse.*

I gratefully acknowledge The Arts Council/An Chomhairle Ealaíon for a generous grant in 1999, and Temple Bar Properties for the use of an artist's studio, also in 1999.